Mr. Smidjet Flips Again

As Seen
Through The
Eyes Of
Mrs. Smidjet
Written by Katie J. Woods
Illustrated by Gordon W. Kelley

Owl Publishing, Inc.

Colton, Oregon 97017

Owl Publishing is a trademark of Owl Publishing, Inc.
.

Published 2014

Cover design by Gordon W. Kelley.

Book design by Katie J. Woods, Gordon W. Kelley.

Printed in United States.

Library of Congress Cataloging-in-pulication Data
Woods, Katie J. 2014
  Mr. Smidjet Flips Again…
  ISBN: 13-978-1500733711
        10-1500733717
  1. Goal (psychology) 2. Self-realization 3. Healing

Two amazing men inspired me to continue my quest to help others by their words, encouragement, and heartfelt kindness. With gratitude and thanksgiving I dedicate, "Mr. Smidjet Flips Again," to Donald Altman and Phil Knight, two angels that taught me to fly.

For You

The One Who Held

My Hand

Wiped My Tears

And Believed In Me

When I Was Lost

Reaching

Out A Hand With Love

My Precious Angel

My Mother, Marian G. Perry

Mr. Smidjet Flips Again

Looking At Bi-polar Illness Through Mrs. Smidjet's Eyes

Katie J. Woods , MS

Once upon a time there was a Smidjet who lived deep in the forest. He was different than any other of the Smidjets, because he was

- Easily distracted
- Had poor judgment
- Had poor temper control/easily agitated
- Had reckless behavior and lack of self control
    - Binge eating
    - Sex with many partners
    - Racing thoughts
    - Talking a lot
    - Low self esteem.
    - Difficulty concentrating, remembering, or making decisions.

Mr. Smidjet realized that he had all of these symptoms, but could not conrol them. As hard as Mr. Smidjet tried, he would lose his temper with Mrs. Smidjet, overeat, get upset over things he misunderstood, talk a lot and interrupt people, and make decisions that were not good for himself and Mrs. Smidjet.   Mrs. Smidjet was often sad and tried her best to make things better, but to no avail. She made his lunches, did his laundry, helped put on his socks and shoes because he couldn't bend over and even dressed him when he was really tired. None of this worked, because he would still yell at her if she disagreed with anything that he said. He had a disease called Bi-polar illness. (Appendix 1)

Several of the animals in the forest tried to talk to Mr. Smidjet about how he had treated Mrs. Smidjet, but he would only get angry and ignore them. One day Mr. Owl flew over to his house and very gently tried to talk to Mr. Smidjet about his temper. The conversation seemed to be going well…but all of a sudden…Mr. Smidjet grabbed his new video camera and shattered it in a million pieces. Mr. Owl was so frightened and he began to flutter around the room. Mr. Smidjet imitated him, which only frightened Mr. Owl more. Finally, Mr. Owl flew through an open window to the shelter of his home vowing he would never visit Mr. Smidjet again.

Mr. Smidjet sat down and cried and cried vowing to not lose his temper again and hating himself for yelling at Mr. Owl and breaking his beautiful camera. He promised himself that he would never yell again…but in less than an hour he broke his promise when Mr. Squirrel came over to talk about how he had treated Mr. Owl. Mr. Smidjet screamed so loud that Mr. Squirrel's tail quivered. He scampered out of the house so fast that part of his fur stuck in Mr. Smidjet's door. Again…Mr. Smidjet sat down and cried and cried vowing to never yell again.

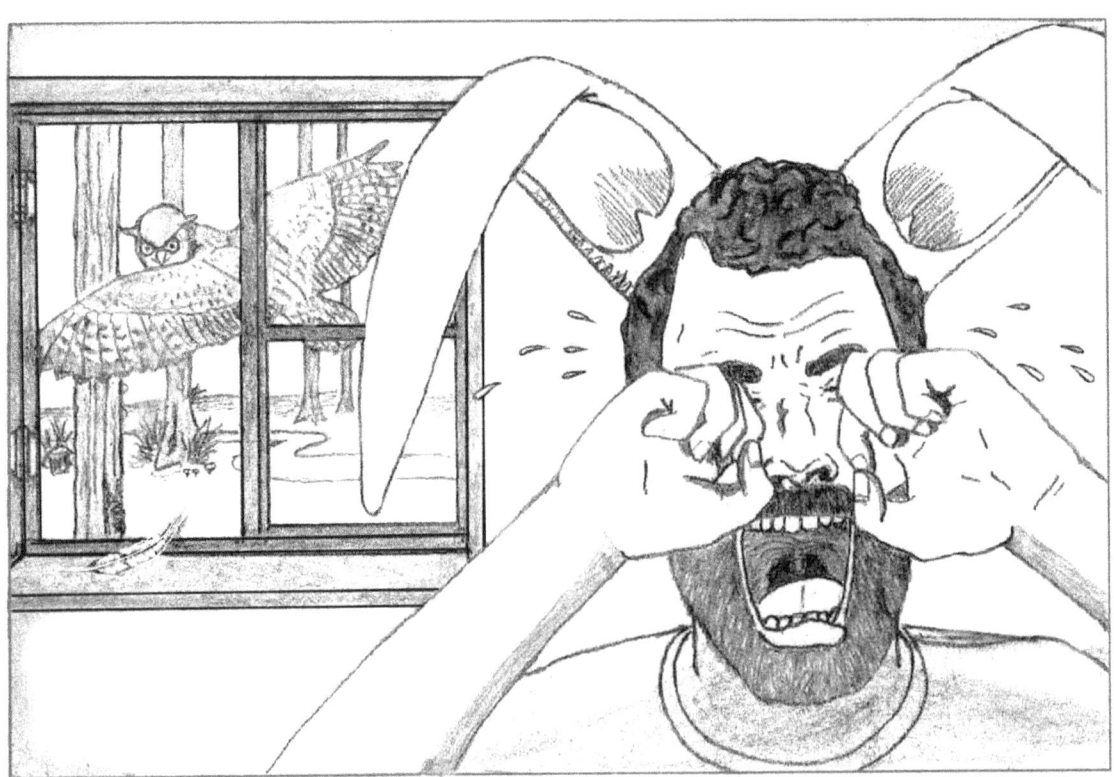

The next day Mr. Smidjet vowed to be much nicer to Mrs. Smidjet. He made her favorite coffee and prepared it just the way she liked it. He told her how much he loved her and he knew that this time his temper had finally gone away. Hours passed and he really thought that his temper would never appear again…but just when he thought things were calm, he received a letter from his ex-wife asking for money that he didn't owe her. He yelled and cursed and forgot his vow not to get angry. Mrs. Smidjet just sat there watching Mr. Smidjet and began to shake her head. She let out a big sigh and decided to take a walk in the forest just to see if Mr. Smidjet even knew she was gone.

Mr. Smidjet sat in his chair for a long time hoping Mrs. Smidjet didn't mind that he lost his temper…he told her he was sorry, but there was no reply. When he looked at her chair, it was empty. "Oh no," cried Mr. Smidjet, "where is Mrs. Smidjet?"

Mr. Smidjet got out of his chair and went into the forest in search of Mrs. Smidjet. He realized his search was in vain without help, and sought the aid of their forest friends. Mrs. Smidjet was nowhere to be found, and with every step he took, he knew that she must have heard what he had said during his angry outburst. Things like, "I wish Mrs. Smidjet was dead, so we would never fight"…"things like there must be another woman that would be better to me." These things were angry lies, and he didn't know why he had thought or said them. Tears fell down his face, and it seemed like a river of pain surrounded him. With every step, he knew he had lost Mrs. Smidjet. His legs grew wearier and wearier, and he gave up finding Mrs. Smidjet and headed for home.

As Mr. Smidjet neared his house, he saw that there was a light on, and he could only hope that Mrs. Smidjet had come back . He loved her so much, and he didn't know why he had said so many mean things to her. It seemed like he could not control himself, and often said angry things that he did not mean. The worst thing about it was that his "fits" usually lasted about two days, and at the end of the two days, Mrs. Smidjet would look sadder than ever. "What was wrong with Mr. Smidjet?" He had to find out, and planned to apologize to Mr. Owl, and ask his advice the very next morning.

Meanwhile Mrs. Smidjet was sitting in her chair patiently waiting for Mr. Smidjet to come home. Mrs Smidjet's walk had helped her to calm down, and she was hoping for a nice evening.

The longer Mrs. Smidjet sat, the more she began to recall all the hurts she had endured during their brief time together. She recalled the first time Mr. Smidjet told her he had cheated on her, and the second, and the third, and the fourth…and so on. Her heart had been broken so many times, but each time she had forgiven Mr. Smidjet knowing that he could not help what he had done.

Mrs. Smidjet also recalled what it was like when she first met Mr. Smidjet. They frolicked and played day after day as though there were no tomorrow…and she knew deep in her heart that he loved her. Everyday was filled with love and laughter, and she hoped it would always be that way.

The first time that Mr. Smidjet yelled at Mrs. Smidjet was the shock of her life. She kept asking why, and he kept getting madder. Later, Mr. Smidjet told her he had cheated, and he was mad at himself.

As she recalled memory after memory, Mrs. Smidjet realized again that whenever she needed help…Mr. Smidjet's temper would take over…and…

One memory particularly stood out…

Things seemed to be going well…but Mrs. Smidjet found out she was very sick…she tried to be brave, but her anxiety grew and grew… and on one particular day, Mrs. Smidjet completely came unglued…she yelled and cried and yelled some more. All of her sadness over the past few years overtook her, and she was terrified. She tried to get a hold of Mr. Smidjet, thinking he would help, but things went from bad to worse, and when he finally came home, instead of comforting her, Mr. Smidjet yelled even louder…

All of Mrs. Smidjet's hope was gone, and she packed her little bag and went to the train station. She didn't want to be any more trouble to Mr. Smidjet…

Mr. Smidjet sat in his chair for a long time not realizing that Mrs. Smidjet had left. When at last he got up from his chair, he called her name over and over, but she did not answer. His heart sank wondering if Mrs. Smidjet was gone.

Mr. Smidjet put on his coat, and walked from house to house crying all the way. He called Mrs. Smidjet's name over and over, but she did not answer back. After what seemed hours, he sat against a tree and fell asleep.

Night came and Mr. Smidjet continued to sleep... dreaming of Mrs. Smidjet and all the plans and dreams they had shared. Why had he yelled at her? What was wrong with him? Why couldn't he control himself? There was no one sweeter or more giving than Mrs. Smidjet, and now she was gone.

Mr. Smidjet began to recall many of his behaviors. Like the time he told Mrs. Smidjet that he didn't like the way she wanted sex. He went on and on for two days telling her that she wasn't romantic enough, didn't give him enough foreplay, and didn't cuddle enough. Mrs. Smidjet didn't know what to do, because for two years he had told her she was perfect with her wild sexcapades, and now he was taking all of her wonderful memories away.

Mr. Smidjet recalled how discouraged Mrs. Smidjet was thinking that she wasn't enough for Mr. Smidjet. As he thought about her sweet face, he felt so sad about how he treated her. He wanted to be kinder, but some sort of monster (bi-polar illness) lived inside of him, and he couldn't seem to treat Mrs. Smidjet with the love she deserved.

On that very same day Mr. Smidjet decided to talk to wise old owl to get some help, but he ended up yelling at him too. Wise old owl was again angry with Mr. Smidjet and told him not to come back. What was wrong with Mr. Smidjet? Why couldn't he control his angry outbursts? Why was he so mean to Mrs. Smidjet…and now to Wise Old Owl?

Mr. Smidjet sat in his chair and cried and cried and cried. He hated the way he had treated "Wise Old Owl," and he knew that his life long friend was his only hope. Mr. Smidjet recalled how "Wise Old Owl" had acted when he was so cruel to him…. His voice had deepened and deepened, his feathers had fluttered, his beady eyes had turned into slits, and he had yelled to the top of his lungs. " Oh, no," said Mr. Smidjet, "Wise Old Owl was acting just like me."

Mr. Smidjet wondered if there was anyone in the world that would help him. Mrs. Smidjet had stuck by him for nearly 3 years, and now she was gone. He had put her through so much, and Mrs. Smidjet hadn't deserved it. Time and again she had come back to Mr. Smidjet, but this time he knew she was done…she had had it. And, in the midst of his despair, he knew he had lost the best friend and lover he could ever hope for.

Mr. Smidjet thought back about another time when he had hurt Mrs. Smidjet. Mr. Smidjet, G-smidjet, and Mrs. Smidjet went out for dinner and during the final course Mr. Smidjet and G-smidjet started talking about hunting. Mr. Smidjet knew deep down that this talk would make Mrs. Smidjet sad, but he didn't want to hurt G-smidjet's feelings. Mrs. Smidjet got up from the table and walked down the road. Again, her heart was broken. She had looked forward to the evening, and she felt unwanted.

Mr. Smidjet continued to talk with G-smidjet and when Mrs. Smidjet returned, they didn't even act like she had been gone. They continued talking "man talk," and Mrs. Smidjet sat crying inside.

When Mr. Smidjet looked up Mrs. Smidjet had left again. "Oh no," Mr. Smidjet said. Why hadn't I realized that Mrs. Smidjet's feelings were hurt and included her in our conversation? Now he knew that Mrs. Smidjet would never come back.

Meanwhile, Mrs. Smidjet sat at the train station trying to figure out what to do. She thought of the countless times Mr. Smidjet had broke her heart, and she didn't want to go through it again. As she sat there, she remembered how she felt each time Mr. Smidjet had let her down.

Mrs. Smidjet particularly remembered the time when Mr. Smidjet's friend came to her house and made fun of her. Mr. Smidjet just stood there and didn't say a word. Time after time Mr. Smidjet's friend had insulted her, and Mr. Smidjet hadn't said anything to defend Mrs. Smidjet. After Mr. Smidjet's friend left, Mr. Smidjet cried and promised that he would always stick up for Mrs. Smidjet. Months went by and Mr. Smidjet had many opportunities, but he did not stick up for Mrs. Smidjet.

Mrs. Smidjet's memories continued to flood over her, and she realized how lonely she was. She so desperately needed a friend, and felt that she didn't have one.   She didn't feel as though Mr. Smidjet loved her. In fact, she wondered why he had even married her. Once upon a time she had so much hope, but it had long since passed. Mrs. Smidjet was lost and had nowhere to go.

It seemed like forever that Mrs. Smidjet had sat in the cold train station trying to figure out what to do. Most of her memories were sad ones, and she really didn't feel like living anymore. She was sick, miserably sad, and felt unloved. She wanted to die, because living had become too painful. At long last, Mrs. Smidjet gave up and fell asleep hoping that her demise would come soon.

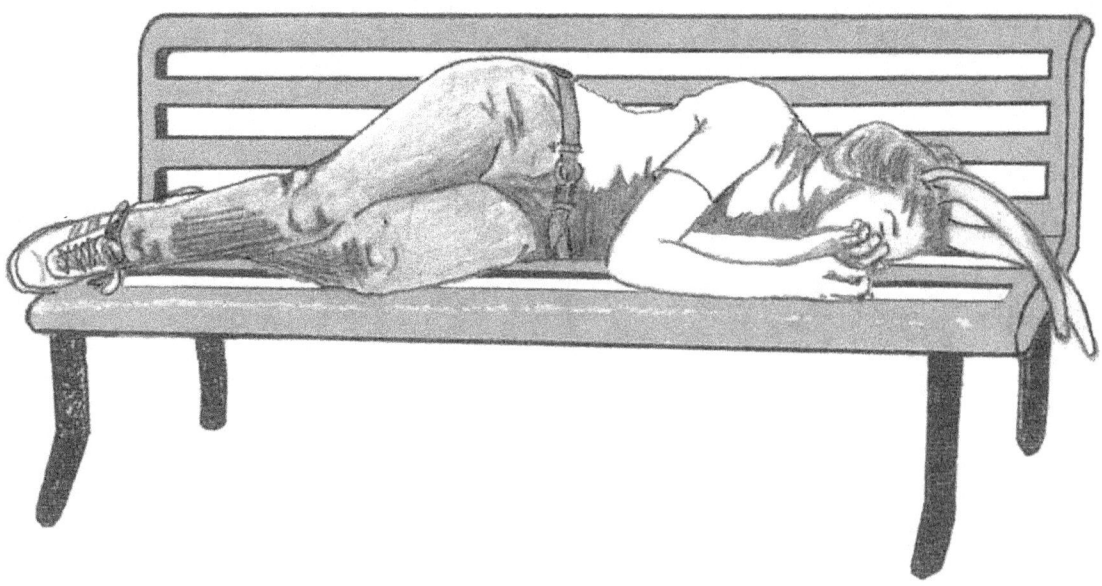

Mrs. Smidjet woke up several hours later feeling somewhat better. She remembered what Mr. Owl had told her about Mr. Smidjet's mental illness. She would never forget the day when he sat Mr. Smidjet down and told him that he had bi-polar illness. At first Mr. Smidjet was extremely angry, but when Mr. Owl read the symptoms for bi-polar illness, Mr. Smidjet had to admit that the diagnosis "fit" him perfectly. (Appendix 1)

Mr. Smidjet put his hands over his face and began to cry. It seemed like he cried for hours, but it was only minutes. The guilt that he felt overcame him, and he was exceedingly sorry for how he had treated Mrs. Smidjet. Oh how he wished he had known what was wrong with him long ago.

Mrs. Smidjet continued to remember how difficult it had been for her to deal with bi-polar illness. Not only did Mr. Smidjet have the symptoms, his son G-smidjet had several including severe mood swings. One day he would be nice to Mrs. Smidjet, and the next he would say terrible things to her causing her to give up

Mrs. Smidjet would never forget the first time that G-smidjet had broken her heart. He started some unbelievable rumors and spread them all through Mr. Smidjet's family. Not only did Mr. Smidjet's family turn on her but also G-smidjet spread the rumors to Mrs. Smidjet's friends at the monastery near by. Mr. Smidjet's family called, the monastery called, and Mrs. Smidjet sat down and put her hands in her face crying harder than she ever had.

What was the purpose of G-smidjet's lies? She had always been kind and loving. Why was this happening to her? Mrs. Smidjet had no idea. She only knew that she had given up and didn't want to go home. She loved Mr. Smidjet, but she couldn't deal with G-smidjet any more.

Mrs. Smidjet continued to sit at the train station. She had spent two days trying to figure out what to do, and she still didn't have an answer. She loved Mr. Smidjet, but she couldn't handle the way she was treated by Mr. Smidjet's family. Gm-smidjet had told her that she didn't care at all about her, that she wasn't welcome in her house, and that she did not want to have anything to do with her. M-smidjet and D-smidjet had told her she just wanted Mr. Smidjet for his money, which was really funny because he didn't have any, and lastly, T-smidjet told Mrs. Smidjet to leave the family during a wedding ceremony.

When she thought about all the things that had happened, Mrs. Smidjet felt lost and lonely...and totally unloved and unprotected. Time after time Mr. Smidjet's family tried to "get rid of her," and no one stood up for her.

The sadness she felt surrounded her, and she longed for her forest friends to give her comfort.

Mrs. Smidjet felt like giving up. She tried to think of some good times that she had with Mr. Smidjet, but as hard as she thought, she couldn't remember very many. But then something came to Mrs. Smidjet's mind, and she remembered a trip to the Umpqua River and another trip to Whidbey Island. It seemed they were best friends, and they could talk about anything. Nothing was too personal, and Mrs. Smidjet felt that they would grow closer and closer. It was as though everything that they touched turned to gold. They had their own little "shoe box" place to stay, and they were happy.

Mrs. Smidjet wished those feelings would come back, but she knew that they wouldn't. She wiped her tears away and started to remember several details that had broken her heart.

- Mrs. Smidjet didn't feel comfortable about talking about personal things/she worried she would make Mr. Smidjet angry.
- Mrs. Smidjet didn't feel that Mr. Smidjet would share his deepest secrets, as he had at the Umpqua River.
- Mrs. Smidjet felt that her trust wasn't the same. Mr. Smidjet had made promises at the Umpqua River, and he had broken several.
- Mrs. Smidjet felt that romantic gestures came and went and she didn't feel she was asking for too much.

Mrs. Smidjet had given Mr. Smidjet so many chances. Each time he broke
his promises he would beg for one more chance, but nothing ever changed.
She tried everything to make Mr. Smidjet happy but nothing worked.

She laid out his clothes; ran his shower, made him popcorn, but he would
not even give her a note. She hinted time and time again but it never
worked, and if she directly ask Mr. Smidjet for any kind of thank you card,
he would get mad and scream at her in an angry outhurst.

Mrs. Smidjet knew that she had to let go, but she didn't know how.
Somehow the train station had seemed the answer, but she still didn't know
how to leave permanently. The only friend that would be able to help her
was Mr. Owl, and he was back in the forest.

Mrs. Smidjet scooped up her little bag and looked for the trail home. When
she came to the edge of the forest it seemed so dark, but she was determined
to find her way. After what seemed an eternity she met Mr. Smidjet sitting
on a log crying. He jumped up and hugggggggggggggged her so hard that
she nearly burst. Mr. Smidjet just kept yelling, "I love you Mrs. Smidjet."

Somehow Mr. Smidjet realized that he was losing "his" Mrs. Smidjet and he
begged her for one last chance to try again.

It seemed like hours…when Mr. Smidjet finally let Mrs. Smidjet go. He was at the bottom of himself, and realized that he could not live without her. He just wanted to "fix" what was broken, and he only knew one friend/counselor that could help.

Mr. Smidjet finally persuaded Mrs. Smidjet to try just one more time. The sad looking pair headed deeper into the forest to find Mr. Owl. At first Mr. Owl would not speak to Mr. Smidjet, but ran around in circles fluttering his feathers and saying horrid things about him. Mr. Smidjet did not know what to do to convince Mr. Owl. All he could do was stand there with his head down and his hands in his pockets crying countless tears.

Mr. Owl gazed up at Mr. Smidjet, and somehow his heart began to melt. He could see that Mr. Smidjet wanted to change, and somehow there had to be a way.

Mr. Owl stood for a long time trying to decide what to do. He finally came to the conclusion that he would indeed help Mr. Smidjet. He gathered several tonics from his herbal concoctions and debated several times as to what would work best for Mr. Smidjet.

- First of all Mr. Smidjet would have to agree to take the medicine that Mr. Owl prescribed.
- Second of all Mr. Smidjet would have to take a precise dose at a precise time.
- And, thirdly, Mr. Smidjet could never miss a dose. (Appendix 2)

Mr. Owl brought out several tried and true remedies, but he knew it would have to be just the right one. He looked at all of them over and over and finally came to the conclusion that lithium carbonate would be just the ticket. He then prescribed three pills a day to be taken at regular intervals.

Next Mr. Owl looked Mr. Smidjet right in the eyes and made him promise to follow all of his instructions.

Mr. Smidjet stammered a wee bit, but then gave a wholehearted yes. He hated his temper among other things that he had suffered from, and he did not want to lose Mrs. Smidjet.

Mr. Owl began writing directions on a very large piece of paper knowing that Mr. Smidjet would have a hard time keeping a medication schedule. With every stroke of his pen he looked right into Mr. Smidjet's eyes making sure that he was not wasting his time. He asked Mr. Smidjet several times if would really take his medicine, and Mr. Smidjet gave a rip roaring yes.

As Mr. Owl made Mr. Smidjet's medicine chart, Mr. Smidjet continued to look sad. He just couldn't figure out why he had treated Mrs. Smidjet so poorly over and over and over. He hadn't wanted to, but time after time he had yelled at her, broke chairs, or raged at her. He was at the bottom of himself and wanted to change.

Mrs. Smidjet had forgiven him over and over, and he knew that this was his last chance, and he didn't want to blow it. Mr. Smidjet also knew that Mr. Owl was right, and he was bi-polar. He hadn't cheated on Mrs. Smidjet for months, but he had shown…

- Angry outbursts
- Uncontrollable rage
- Reckless behavior

Each one of his symptoms showed signs of bi-polar illness, and he could only hope that Mr. Owl was right and lithium would work. (Appendix 1)

When it came time to leave, Mr. Smidjet went into Mr. Owl's library to pick up Mrs. Smidjet only to find her fast asleep in Mr. Owl's rocking chair. She looked so exhausted, and Mr. Smidjet began to cry. He had put Mrs. Smidjet through so much and he did not deserve her forgiveness or her love, but he wanted to try again and somehow he knew that if he did exactly what Mr. Owl said that he would win Mrs. Smidjet back.

Mr. Smidjet gently woke Mrs. Smidjet and put his arm around her hoping they could make it back to their home without Mrs. Smidjet collapsing.

As they walked Mr. Smidjet told Mrs. Smidjet over and over how much he loved her and wanted to change. He told her what Mr. Owl prescribed, and he promised at least 23 times that he would never yell or rage at her.

When the weary couple finally arrived at their little home in the forest, they fell onto their beds without even undressing. Just before falling asleep Mr. Smidjet jumped up and took his first lithium pill. He was certain he would never forget the most important part of his life.

When he came back to bed, Mr. Smidjet undressed Mrs. Smidjet and put her favorite comforter on her. She looked so weary and simply let out a sigh. Mr. Smidjet knew that his new medicine would not help every part of their life, but he was determined to try.

The next morning Mrs. Smidjet had an odd feeling when Mr. Smidjet began to talk about a particular road he had been on. Mr. Smidjet seemed somewhat defensive, but she didn't say anything hoping the feeling would go away.

A few hours later Mr. Smidjet dropped Mrs. Smidjet off at Mr. Crow's house promising to pick her up at 12:00. A short time passed, and Mrs. Smidjet felt her tummy growl, and she became sicker and sicker. She tried to get hold of Mr. Smidjet…but her symptoms got worse and worse.

Finally, when Mr. Smidjet returned, Mrs. Smidjet was having an anxiety attack and asked Mr. Smidjet where he had been. Mrs. Smidjet could not believe how angry Mr. Smidjet became because things had been going so well. As the evening went on Mr. Smidjet got angrier and angrier and finally Mrs. Smidjet sat down and cried and cried and cried. She had completely given up again. All of the hope that she had was gone, and she just wanted to run away and hide.

Mrs. Smidjet sat and thought of all the ways she could end her life. It was just too hard living with Mr. Smidjet. She had tried everything she could, but she had given up. Every time she was down Mr. Smidjet yelled at her. He just didn't seem to know what to do to comfort her…and she could no longer stay.

Mrs. Smidjet packed her bags and decided to leave Mr. Smidjet for good. As she put each piece of clothing into her little bag, she shed tears of sadness. She had done the best that she could, but she could not go on.

Mrs. Smidjet looked around their little home and recalled memories that she had long forgotten…like the first kiss…and the way Mr. Smidjet used to hold her and tell her how much he loved her. Every moment together meant something special, but those things had long ago passed, and no matter how Mrs. Smidjet tried, she could not bring back the love that she once shared. She had given all that she had, and today she knew the feeling of defeat.

Mrs. Smidjet walked around their tiny little house trying not to forget anything. She looked at the tiny couch where Mr. Smidjet used to hold her so long ago, and the tiny bedroom where they had snuggled during the long winters. Every memory made her sadder, and she had to get away before her heart would break any further.

Finally, Mrs. Smidjet was ready to go. She knew that she may not return, and in a moment of panic frantically looked for the last love note that Mr. Smidjet wrote her. He told her how much he loved her, how wonderful she was, and how he would be lost without her. She didn't feel like Mr. Smidjet's note was real, and as she slammed their little door for the last time a foreboding feeling came over her.

Mrs. Smidjet had been so upset when she left that she didn't realize how dark it was getting. As she tried to make it through the forest, she stumbled over a log on the path. She didn't know what to do. Darkness had set in, and everytime she tried to get up, she stumbled back onto the path. Finally in desperation, she layed down and cried herself to sleep.

After what seemed an eternity, she heard a voice whispering, "Mrs. Smidjet," I'm here. Mrs. Smidjet thought she must be dreaming, but then she realized it was Mr. Squirrel. "Mrs. Smidjet you have fallen, and your ankle is swollen. We are going to make a splint and help you to safety." Mrs. Smidjet wondered who "we were"…but in that moment Mr. Owl came with a lantern, and all of her forest friends were there to help her. She had never felt so loved.

Somehow in a matter of minutes all of her friends made a stretcher to take her to Mr. Squirrel's home. "One, two three," they loaded Mrs. Smidjet up, and gently carried her to the warmth of Mr. Squirrel's home.

When she got there she couldn't believe her eyes. A warm fire was laid in the hearth, and she could smell cider. As softly as a feather, she was lifted off her stretcher and placed on the couch in front of the cozy fire...

The next morning Mrs. Smidjet awoke to the smell of fresh baked biscuits. She blinked her eyes several times forgetting where she was but soon realized that she was in Mr. Squirrel's home. She hadn't felt this safe in a very long time, and she laid her head back on her pillow content to be alive.

Within minutes Mr. Squirrel brought her a beautiful breakfast tray filled with fruit, eggs benedict, and fresh biscuits and jam. No one had ever treated Mrs. Smidjet so well, and she began to cry. Mr. Squirrel gently wiped her tears away and in a very soft voice said, "you are loved Mrs. Smidjet."

Mrs. Smidjet savored every bit of her breakfast and laid back against her pillow and fell back asleep. When she awoke for a second time, Mrs. Smidjet noticed that her clothes were laid out at the bottom of her bed. It was so hard for her to believe that anyone would treat her this kindly, but it was happening, and a small smile creased her lips.

Mrs. Smidjet climbed out of bed and began to dress having no idea that her clothes had been warmed by Mr. Squirrel. She wondered how Mr. Squirrel had kept them warm, but she dare not ask for being rude. Mrs. Smidjet simply sat on the edge of her bed so thankful to be cared for. She had always been the caretaker, and it felt strange for someone to be caring for her.

Mrs. Smidjet climbed out of bed with a spring in her step. She not only felt excited…she felt elated. She had lived in fear of Mr. Smidjet for so long that she had not realized how it would feel if she was loved and cared for without anger.

Mr. Squirrel peeked his head in Mrs. Smidjet's room to see if she needed anything else. His smile was precious to Mrs. Smidjet because it had been so long since she felt someone really cared.

Mrs. Smidjet finished dressing and walked slowly into the kitchen where Mr. Squirrel was reading his paper. He patted the seat next to him, and Mrs. Smidjet sank deeply into the cushioned chair. Without notice Mrs. Smidjet began to cry. No one had ever treated her so wonderfully, and her emotions overcame her. She wondered if she might be dreaming, and if she was, she never wanted to wake up.

Mr. Squirrel's face softened when he saw Mrs. Smidjet's tears. He had wanted to make her feel loved, and now she was crying. He gently patted her face with a warm towel, and gingerly stroked her hand telling her that it would be all right.

Mrs. Smidjet couldn't believe how kind she was being treated, and at that moment, she decided that she never wanted to leave Mr. Squirrel's house. She tried to tell Mr. Squirrel how she felt, but her tears overtook her thoughts, and all she could do was cry.

Mr. Squirrel quietly put his arm around Mrs. Smidjet's shoulders and told her she would never be afraid again, and it was OK to cry. For what seemed like hours, Mr. Squirrel and Mrs. Smidjet sat in silence enjoying each other's company knowing that nothing needed to be said.

For the first time in Mrs. Smidjet's life, she knew what it was to feel loved. She had never felt so secure and wondered if she could spend the rest of her life with Mr. Squirrel.

Before that peaceful thought had time to sink into Mrs. Smidjet's mind, there was a knock at the door. There stood Mr. Crow talking so fast that Mrs. Smidjet could not understand what he was saying. "Mr. Smidjet is hurt…hurt…hurt." Mr. Squirrel gently spoke to Mr. Crow trying to calm him down. Finally, Mr. Crow spoke clearly and told Mrs. Smidjet that Mr. Smidjet had fallen from a tree and was asking for Mrs. Smidjet.

Within minutes, Mr. Crow, Mrs. Smidjet, and Mr. Squirrel were out the door and headed into the forest to find Mr. Smidjet. It seemed like they had walked miles when they heard a moan coming from the forest. The closer they got, the louder the moan became. Just as they turned the corner, there was Mr. Smidjet lying on the ground beneath a large(secluded) tree in the forest.

Mrs. Smidjet quickly ran over to comfort Mr. Smidjet. She gently stroked his forehead trying to ease his pain, Mr. Smidjet awoke for a few seconds, and a tiny smile creased his lips. He let out a sigh and fell back to sleep.

Mrs. Smidjet sat on the ground next to Mr. Smidjet trying to be of comfort to Mr. Smidjet. She sang to him, told him his favorite stories, and continued to stroke his head. As she tenderly nursed him, a fear she had never felt overcame her, "had Mr. Smidjet purposely harmed himself to win her back." Only Wise Old Owl and her supportive friends would help her find the answer to this mystery.

As Mr. Squirrel watched Mrs. Smidjet with Mr. Smidjet, he knew that she would not go home with him again. He would always treasure their memories, but his heart told him that they would just be memories.

Mrs. Smidjet continued to stroke Mr. Smidjet seeming to have forgotten how he had treated her. Mr. Smidjet looked so fragile, and she just wanted to take care of him. It had been wonderful to have Mr. Squirrel take care of her, but now she knew what she must do.

Mr. Owl arrived with potions to save Mr. Smidjet. He tried one and then another and finally found just the right one. Mr. Smidjet awoke with a start, crying as hard as he ever had. Mrs. Smidjet was right next to him, and he knew that everything would be all right.

Mrs. Smidjet tried as hard as she could to soothe Mr. Smidjet, but he only cried louder. He had been so lonely without Mrs. Smidjet, and now they were finally together. He never wanted her to go away again, but he was so afraid he would continue to lose his temper. Mr. Owl had changed his medication more than once, and Mr. Smidjet finally felt calm, but he knew that his anger would come back if he wasn't careful.

None of the previous perscriptions worked except for Mr. Owl's new medication, Gabapentin. Mr. Owl told Mr. Smidjet that it was important that he take the medication that was right for him. (Appendix 3).

Mr. Smidjet continued to cry and Mrs. Smidjet continued to soothe him. After what seemed an eternity, Mr. Smidjet calmed down and let out a huge sigh. His beloved Mrs. Smidjet was back, and he never wanted to lose her again.

Mrs. Smidjet tried to figure out how to get Mr. Smidjet home. She knew she couldn't do it by herself, and would need the help of several of her forest friends. She asked Mr. Badjer to spread the word, and one by one help arrived.

Mr. Owl organized the group giving each one a specific duty. In only a few minutes, the materials for Mr. Smidjet's stretcher arrived, and the sound of hammering echoed throughout the forest.

Mr. Badger placed the stretcher right next to Mr. Smidjet, and each one of his friends gave a shove at the sound of three. As the small band of friends trekked through the forest, Mr. Smidjet laid back content knowing he was going home.

When they arrived at Mr. and Mrs. Smidjet's home, all the animals laid the stretcher right next to Mr. Smidjet's bed and gently moved him. Mr. Smidjet was finally safe, and his heart could barely hold the joy that he felt. He was home, Mrs. Smidjet was with him, and his life would be forever happy if he could continue to hold his temper.

Mrs. Smidjet gently took off Mr. Smidjet's clothes and put his pajamas on. As she tiptoed out of their bedroom, she heard Mr. Smidjet quietly saying that he was the luckiest man in the world.

After thanking all of her forest friends, Mrs. Smidjet sighed and began to make Mr.Smidjet some hot chocolate and his favorite muffins.

Days passed... and slowly Mr. Smidjet began to heal. Each day Mrs. Smidjet tenderly nursed him… stroking his forehead and telling Mr. Smidjet his favorite stories. Mr. Smidjet seemed happier than he ever had because he felt truly loved. After all he had put Mrs. Smidjet through, she was still in his life loving him and nursing Mr. Smidjet back to health.

After what seemed an eternity, Mr. Smidjet was able to climb out of his bed. The first thing that he did was give Mrs. Smidjet the biggest hug he could possibly muster. She seemed to sink into his arms, and he knew they would always be happy. Mr. Smidjet also knew that he would always have to take his medication and see Mr. Owl on a regular basis to keep Mrs. Smidjet.

Mr. and Mrs. Smidjet continued to be happy for days…but on the 13th. day G-smidjet came by and wanted to talk to Mr. Smidjet by himself. G-smidjet told Mr. Smidjet all the things that he hated about Mrs. Smidjet knowing that Mr. Smidjet wouldn't say a word.

What G-smidjet didn't realize was that Mr. Smidjet had decided to never let G-smidjet put anyone down again…let alone Mrs. Smidjet. Mr. Smidjet stood up as tall as he could…raised his chest to it's full extent…and let out a scream so loud that several of Mr. Smidjet's forest friends came running to see what was happening. When they saw that G-smidjet was being put in his place, they all cheered.

Mr. Smidjet repeated the same words over and over, "YOU WILL NEVER BE MEAN TO MRS. SMIDJET AGAIN. YOU WILL NEVER TALK BEHIND HER BACK…YOU WILL NEVER HURT HER FEELINGS…IF YOU DO…I WILL NEVER TALK TO YOU.

G-Smidjet was so shocked that he began to walk backwards talking under his breath. All the animals escorted him out of Mr. and Mrs. Smidjet's house, and Mr. Smidjet yelled, "I'll call you in a week."

Mr. Smidjet flopped down into his chair totally exhausted at what he had just done. Never again would Mr. Smidjet let anyone harm Mrs. Smidjet in any way.

Mr. Smidjet took the longest nap that he had ever taken in his life, and when he awoke, he wrote a list of what he had to do to be the husband that Mrs. Smidjet needed. He entitled it, "List 1."

How Else Can I Manage Bipolar Disorder?

- Take my medication.
- See my therapist regularly.
- Learn more about bipolar disorder and its treatment
- Participate in a support group
- Adopt healthy habits, including exercising, practicing stress management techniques, eating healthy, avoiding alcohol and drugs, getting seven to eight hours of sleep and avoiding any potential triggers. (Appendix 2)

Mr. Smidjet knew that if he took his medication and followed his list, he would always be happy with Mrs. Smidjet.

Mr. Smidjet read and re-read his list wanting to make sure that he didn't forget anything. In his heart he knew if he protected Mrs. Smidjet and followed it, nothing would happen to stand in their way of their happiness.

He also knew that he had to be especially careful when G-smidjet came around. He had hurt Mrs. Smidjet in so many ways, but Mr. Smidjet was steadfast and firmly planted with the idea that no one would hurt Mrs. Smidjet again.

Mr. Smidjet lay in his bed knowing that he would always be cared for as long as he placed Mrs. Smidjet first in his life...something he had never done.

In the distance, Mr. Smidjet could hear Mrs. Smidjet puttering around in the kitchen making his dinner. He knew that he was the luckiest Smidjet in the forest, and nothing was going to change that.

Just when he thought he couldn't be happier, Mrs. Smidjet arrived with a hot steaming bowl of soup, a huge platter of corn bread, and a hot cup of coffee. As Mrs. Smidjet placed it on Mr. Smidjet's serving table, she reached down and gently kissed Mr. Smidjet's forehead. Mr. Smidjet let out a big sigh and began to eat his supper knowing that he was truly loved.

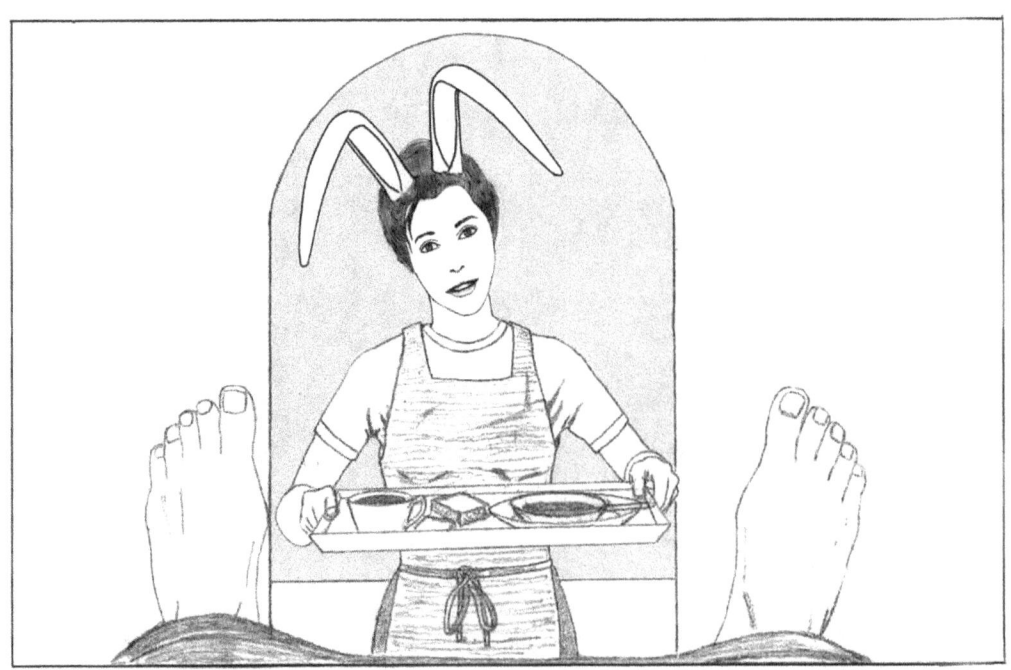

Days followed into weeks, and Mr. and Mrs. Smidjet continued to live peacefully in their little house in the forest. Mr. Smidjet's health returned as Mrs. Smidjet happily cared for him. They took long walks in the forest, both knowing that their life would always be happy.

Each day was a new adventure, and Mr. and Mrs. Smidjet felt like "all was right in their world." Mr. Smidjet's medicine was working, and there had been no signs of bi-polar illness, and Mr. Smidget's temper was gone.

Mr. and Mrs. Smidjet's days couldn't have been brighter, and they knew they would be happy forever.

The next morning Mrs. Smidjet woke up with a strange feeling. For days she and Mr. Smidjet had been happy, but something didn't feel right.

Later that afternoon, when they went for a walk Mrs. Smidjet tried to make the foreboding feeling go away. She complimented Mr. Smidjet numerous times, but his response was different than it had been. In desperation, Mrs. Smidjet talked about trivial things, but Mr. Smidjet changed the subject and angrily replied that he was nothing but a person who took Mrs. Smidjet places. Mrs. Smidjet felt so hurt that she began to cry. This made Mr. Smidjet even madder, and he yelled at her. It was then that she knew that something was very wrong.

When they returned from their walk, Mrs. Smidjet busied herself in the kitchen hoping that Mr. Smidjet's mood would go away. Somehow she had to make it through the day.

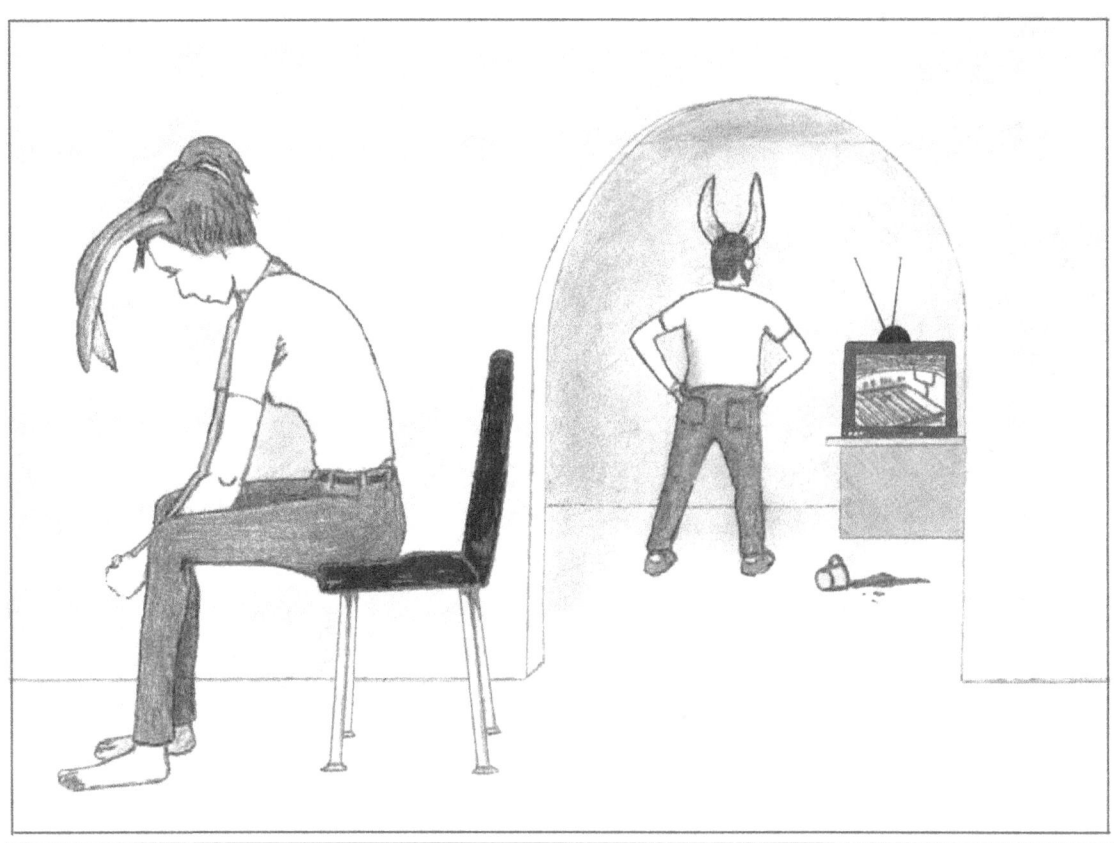

Morning came, and Mrs. Smidjet's feelings turned from concerned to ominous. She tried every way she knew how to talk to Mr. Smidjet about what had happened, but he fired back at her with an angry retort saying, "Mrs. Smidjet was ruining his business, never listened to him, and always tried to run his life."

When things felt like they couldn't get worse, Mrs. Smidjet heard a knock at the door. She scurried to the door and to her disappointment there stood not one but three G-smidjets. She held her breath hoping she could get through their visit, but knowing that she would be ignored by all of them including Mr. Smidjet.

All the work that Mrs. Smidjet had put into helping Mr.Smidjet convalesce was to no avail. The nurturing, love, and kindness was unappreciated, and Mrs. Smidjet realized how miserable her life was.

Tears came, and they were like a flood of grief…the grief of trying for over two years and having nothing work. She kept expecting Mr. Smidjet to say something nice, but instead she heard angry words that put her down.

When Mrs. Smidjet went to bed she got down on her knees and prayed that she could figure out what was wrong. Her little heart was broken, and she wanted "her" Mr. Smidjet back. What could she do?

Later, when Mr. Smidjet came to bed, she noticed that he had an extra gabapentin in his hand and asked him how long he had been taking 4 pills instead of three. Finally…there was her answer. Mr. Owl had told them that it was very important that they follow the directions on the Gabapentin bottle and take only what was prescribed. How had Mrs. Smidjet let this happen? Why hadn't Mrs Smidjet watched over Mr. Smidjet more closely? It was at that very moment that she realized that she had to help Mr. Smidjet remember his medication and they had to become a team. (Appendix 2)

When Mr. Smidjet woke up, Mrs. Smidjet was careful not to say anything that would bother him. She only said nice things, and as the day went on, she noticed that Mr. Smidjet was saying nice things back.

The hours passed, and Mrs. Smidjet began to experience the ominous feeling that she had a few days before. She tried to make it go away, but to no avail. Finally, Mrs. Smidjet read a book and tried to make her uncomfortableness subside.

Just when Mrs. Smidjet was beginning to relax, there was a knock at the door. Just as before, it was G-smidjet. Mr. Smidjet and G-smidjet talked and talked barely paying attention to Mrs. Smidjet. Somehow her little heart couldn't handle being ignored again, and she quietly crept into the forest. With each step of the way Mrs. Smidjet cried and cried knowing that she had done her best, but also knowing that she would never fit in.

About an hour later Mr. Smidjet looked around wondering where Mrs. Smidjet was. Suddenly he realized what had happened, and began to cry. Why hadn't he invited Mrs. Smidjet to join the conversation? He promised her that he would. Why didn't he make Mrs. Smidjet feel loved? She had nursed him back to health and taken such good care of him, and he had let her down again.

Meanwhile Mrs. Smidjet continued to make her way through the forest looking for the path that led to the train station She realized she had done her best, but she could no longer stay with Mr. Smidjet. Darkness fell, and nothing looked right. The further she walked, the harder it was to see. Somehow she had lost her way.

To make matters worse, a storm began to brew and Mrs. Smidjet became even more confused. The forest became darker and darker, and the wind and rain nearly knocked Mrs. Smidjet down. Finally, in desperation she sat under a tree.

When Mrs. Smidjet thought that things could not get any worse, a branch fell and knocked her down. As she lay there with her head bleeding, a strong arm lifted her up. To her surprise, it was Mr. Smidjet. "I'm here…lay against me Mrs. Smidjet. I was such a fool. I am so very sorry."

Mr. Smidjet's face was full of tears, and he looked at Mrs. Smidjet with all the love he had in his heart. Over and over, he told her how much he loved her and how sorry he was. Mrs. Smidjet looked up at Mr. Smidjet and she knew how much she truly loved him. They had been through so much, but at that very moment she was safe in Mr. Smidjet's arms.

Mrs. Smidjet would be forever grateful that Mr. Smidjet rescued her from the storm, but she also realized they had a lot of things to work on.

After what seemed like an eternity, Mrs. Smidjet climbed out of her little bed and went to talk to Mr. Smidjet. He looked so sweet sleeping in his big chair, and it was hard for her to wake him up.

Mrs. Smidjet looked deep into Mr. Smidjet's eyes pledging her love to him but letting him know she was going away for a while. All the armies (bi-polar illness) had sought to slay her, and they had finally won. She was exhausted and couldn't go on. 3 1/2 years had passed and nothing had really changed.

Mrs. Smidjet put on her winter coat and ventured out into the forest. It was dark but she wasn't scared anymore because she knew she had to learn to take care of herself.

Appendix 1

The primary symptoms of bipolar disorder are periods of elevated or irritable mood accompanied by dramatic increases in energy, activity, and thinking. The illness has two (bi) strongly contrasting phases (polar): I) bipolar mania or hypo-mania and 2) depression.

I) Bipolar mania or hypo-mania symptoms include:

• Euphoria or irritability
• Increased energy and activity
• Excessive talk; racing thoughts
• Inflated self-esteem
• Unusual energy; less need for sleep
• Impulsiveness, a reckless pursuit of gratification (shopping sprees, impetuous travel, more and sometimes promiscuous sex, high-risk business investments, fast driving)

2) Bipolar depression/major depression symptoms include:

• Depressed mood and low self-esteem
• Low energy levels and apathy
• Sadness, loneliness, helplessness, guilt
• Slow speech, fatigue, and poor coordination
• Insomnia or oversleeping
• Suicidal thoughts and feelings
• Poor concentration
• Lack of interest or pleasure in usual activities

Appendix 2

Tips For Managing Bi-polar Illness

- Take medication prescribed
- See therapist regularly
- Learn more about bi-polar illness and it's treatment
  .
- Participate in a support group.
  a. *www.dbsalliance.org/*
  b. *www.nami.org/*
  c. *www.dbsaoregon.org/**supportgroup**.html*
  d. *psychcentral.com*
  e. *http://psychcentral.com/resources/Bipolar/Support_Groups/*

- Adopt healthy eating habits, including exercising, practicing stress management techniques, eat healthy, avoid alcohol and drugs, get seven to eight hours of sleep and avoid any potential triggers.

Appendix 3

Medication Used for Bipolar Disorder

Mood stabilizers. These medications are prescribed to help stabilize manic symptoms, prevent future episodes and reduce suicide risk. The most well-known of these is lithium, which is effective in 60 to 80 percent of manic and hypomanic episodes. Anticonvulsant (or anti-seizure) medications also have mood stabilizing effects. These include valproate (Depakote), carbamazepine (Tegretol), lamotrigine (Lamictal), gabapentin (Neurotin) and topiramate (Topamax).

Other Medications Commonly Used For Bi-polar Illness

- Zoloft
- Lithium
- Risperidol
- Ametrytyline

Sometimes
At
The

Most
Unexpected
Moment

A
Tiny
Glimpse

Of
Hope
Arrives

Fully
Wrapped
And

Waiting
To
Be opened..